KANGAROOS

by Tanya Lee Stone

BLACKBIRCH®
PRESS

THOMSON
————— ✳ —————™
GALE

San Diego • Detroit • New York • San Francisco • Cleveland • New Haven, Conn. • Waterville, Maine • London • Munich

© 2003 by Blackbirch Press™. Blackbirch Press™ is an imprint of The Gale Group, Inc., a division of Thomson Learning, Inc.

Blackbirch Press™ and Thomson Learning™ are trademarks used herein under license.

For more information, contact
The Gale Group, Inc.
27500 Drake Rd.
Farmington Hills, MI 48331-3535
Or you can visit our Internet site at http://www.gale.com

Photographs © 1991 by Chang Yi-Wen

Cover Photograph © Corbis

© 1991 by Chin-Chin Publications Ltd.

No. 274-1, Sec.1 Ho-Ping E. Rd., Taipei, Taiwan, R.O.C.
Tel: 886-2-2363-3486 Fax: 886-2-2363-6081

LIBRARY OF CONGRESS CATALOGING-IN-PUBLICATION DATA

Stone, Tanya Lee.
  Kangaroos / by Tanya Lee Stone.
    v. cm. -- (Wild wild world)
  Includes bibliographical references (p. 24).
  Contents: Kinds of kangaroos -- Eating and drinking -- Defense --
  Growing up.
    ISBN 1-41030-032-3 (hardback : alk. paper)
    1. Kangaroos--Juvenile literature. [1. Kangaroos.] I. Title. II.
  Series.

  QL737.M35 S753 2003
  599.2'22--dc21
                                                                2002154167

Printed in Taiwan
10 9 8 7 6 5 4 3 2 1

Table of Contents

Kinds of Kangaroos

Kangaroos live in Australia, New Guinea, and nearby islands.

There are many different kinds of kangaroos. The two main large kangaroos are the red and the gray.

Kangaroos are a type of mammal called a marsupial. Marsupials give birth to babies that are not fully developed. They need to finish growing in their mothers' pouches.

Kangaroos do not run like other animals. They hop!

They have very large back feet to push off the ground. Their long tails help them balance.

Large kangaroos can jump more than 20 feet and hop more than 30 miles per hour!

Kangaroo Senses

Kangaroos are always on the lookout for danger.

They have large dark eyes and can see very well.

Their big ears can swivel in any direction to pick up the slightest sound. They also have a strong sense of smell.

Kangaroos often gather in a group called a mob. But if they sense trouble, each kangaroo will hop off by itself. Only mothers and babies stick together.

Eating and Drinking

Most kangaroos are plant eaters.
They mainly eat grass, but they will
eat other plant materials, too.
Kangaroos spend most of the day
grazing and eating. When walking
slowly to graze, they use all four limbs.

They have two large, sharp front
teeth on the bottom and lots of sharp
top teeth for clipping the grass.

Kangaroos like to drink water, even though they get much of the water they need from the plants they eat.

9

Kangaroo Cleaning

Kangaroos like to keep clean. They take great care to wash themselves by licking their paws and rubbing them all over their fur. A kangaroo may even take a bath in a pond or river.

Kangaroos use their front and back claws to comb their wooly fur.

Their back paws each have a toe with two nails close together that are used like tweezers to pick bugs out of their fur.

A Kangaroo Day

Kangaroos graze for food in the morning and again in the evening.

They spend the hottest part of the day sleeping.

There isn't much shade where kangaroos live in the wild.

Sometimes, a kangaroo will dig a shallow hole in the ground to help stay cool.

Defense

Kangaroos are peaceful animals, but they fight when they need to.

These red kangaroos are the largest marsupials. They stand more than 7 feet tall!

A kick from one of these powerful animals can hurt an enemy such as an Australian wild dog called a dingo.

Two male kangaroos will also fight to compete for a female. They stand up tall on their hind feet and fight like boxers.

Mating

When a female is ready to mate, a male will follow her away from the mob.

A male may check the inside of a female's pouch before mating. Mating can last a few hours or a few days. When it is over, the male and female go their separate ways.

The male does not stay with the female to help her raise her young.

Little Joeys

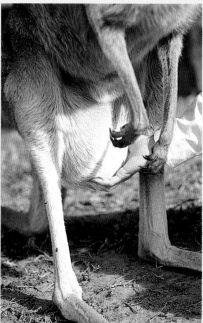

Marsupial babies are not fully developed when they are born.

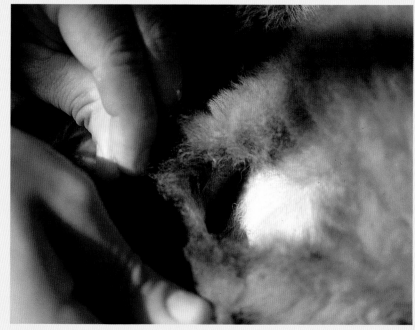

A female marsupial has a pouch on the outside of her body. Her baby finishes growing in the pouch until it can survive outside.

A female kangaroo takes great care to clean her pouch before a baby is born.

A baby kangaroo is called a joey. A joey is tiny at birth, weighing less than an ounce. It is about the size of a peanut.

As soon as it is born, the blind, furless baby crawls through its mother's fur and finds her pouch. Safe inside, a joey drinks its mother's milk and grows.

Growing Up

A joey is not ready to leave its mother's pouch until it is about 6 months old.

By this time, the baby is fully developed.

For a few months after it leaves the pouch, a young kangaroo stays close to its mother.

The joey eats grass, but also pokes its head inside the pouch to nurse.

It will even jump into the pouch headfirst if it gets scared and is still small enough to fit!

By the time it is 2 years old, a kangaroo is ready to live on its own.

The Kangaroo Collection

There are several kinds of kangaroos in many sizes.

The animals shown on the top of the opposite page are red and gray kangaroos.

On the bottom left is a small animal called a musky rat kangaroo. To its right are medium-sized kangaroos called rock wallabies.

There is nothing else on earth quite like a kangaroo.

For More Information

Ivy, Bill. *Kangaroos*. Danbury, CT: Grolier, 1990.

Markle, Sandra. *Outside and Inside Kangaroos*. New York: Atheneum, 1999.

Woodward, John. *Endangered Kangaroos*. New York: Marshall Cavendish, 1997.

Glossary

joey a baby kangaroo

marsupial an animal that gives birth to undeveloped young that need to spend the first part of their lives growing inside their mothers' pouches

mob a group of kangaroos